$19.95

Ar pts

0.5

W9-BBP-915

Carly Rae Jepsen

ABDO
Publishing Company

Big Buddy BOOKS
Buddy Bios

by Sarah Tieck

VISIT US AT
www.abdopublishing.com

Published by ABDO Publishing Company, PO Box 398166, Minneapolis, Minnesota 55439.

Printed in the United States of America, North Mankato, Minnesota.
052013
092013

 PRINTED ON RECYCLED PAPER

Coordinating Series Editor: Rochelle Baltzer
Contributing Editors: Megan M. Gunderson, Marcia Zappa
Graphic Design: Maria Hosley
Cover Photograph: *AP Photo*: Evan Agostini/Invision.
Interior Photographs/Illustrations: *AP Photo*: Agencia EL UNIVERSAL/Rebeca Argumedo. EGV. (GDA via AP Images) (p. 15), Scott Gries (p. 19), Arthur Mola (pp. 5, 9, 11), Rex Features via AP Images (pp. 19, 29), Caroline Seidel/picture-alliance/dpa (p. 19), Jonathan Short, file (p. 12), Charles Sykes/Invision (pp. 21, 23, 27), Ian West/PA URN: 13333243 (Press Association via AP Images) (p. 25), CP PHOTO/Adrian Wyld (p. 11); *Getty Images*: Jeff Fusco (p. 7), Kevin Mazur/WireImage (p. 17); *Shutterstock*: Josef Hanus (p. 9).

Library of Congress Control Number: 2012956007

Cataloging-in-Publication Data

Tieck, Sarah.
 Carly Rae Jepsen: pop star / Sarah Tieck.
 p. cm. -- (Big buddy biographies)
ISBN 978-1-61783-858-3
1. Jepsen, Carly Rae, 1985- --Juvenile literature. 2. Singers--Canada--Biography--Juvenile literature.   I. Title.
782.42164092--dc23
 [B]   2012956007

Contents

Pop Star

Carly Rae Jepsen is a singer and songwriter. She has **released** popular music. Fans around the world enjoy her songs. She is best known for the song "Call Me Maybe."

Carly Rae has appeared in magazines. And, she has been a guest on popular television shows.

Family Ties

Where in the World?

CANADA

British Columbia

Mission

Alberta

UNITED STATES

Washington

Montana

Oregon

Idaho

PACIFIC OCEAN

N W E S

Carly Rae Jepsen is from Canada. She was born in Mission, British Columbia, on November 21, 1985. Carly Rae's parents are Alexandra Lanzarotta and Larry Jepsen. Her stepparents are Ron Lanzarotta and Patty Jepsen. Her brother is Colin and her sister is Katie.

Carly Rae grew up in a family that loved music. Her mother taught her words to songs. And her father would sing to her as she fell asleep. One of her favorite singers was James Taylor.

Carly Rae's look and style have changed over the years.

School Years

Carly Rae went to Heritage Park Secondary School in Mission. She appeared in **musicals** at her school. When she was 17, she got her first **guitar**.

After finishing school, Carly Rae started to **perform** her music in Vancouver. She attended the Canadian College of Performing Arts in Victoria. There, she worked to grow her talent in music.

Carly Rae considered becoming a music teacher.

Vancouver is one of British Columbia's major cities. More than 2 million people live there and in smaller cities nearby.

Starting Out

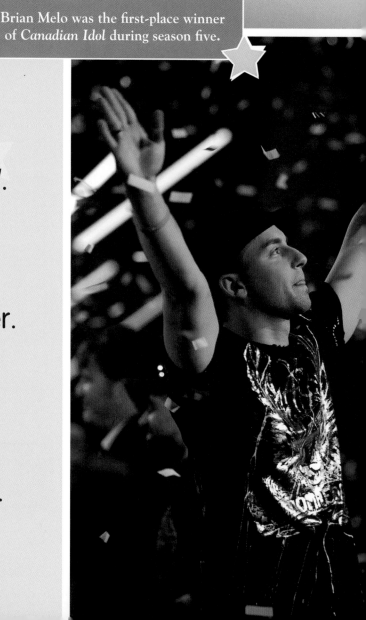

In 2007, Carly Rae appeared on season five of *Canadian Idol*. This popular television show began in 2003. Each season, young people **compete** to be named the best Canadian singer.

Carly Rae tried out. Soon, she and a group of finalists were chosen to **perform** on the show. Each week, Carly Rae and other finalists sang and viewers voted. Carly Rae won third place!

After the show, Carly Rae joined the Canadian Idol Top 3 Tour.

Did you know...

Season five of *Canadian Idol* had a new rule. Singers were allowed to play an instrument when they tried out. Carly Rae played her guitar.

First Album

After *Canadian Idol*, Carly Rae wrote and recorded songs. She worked on forming her music's sound and style.

In 2008, Carly Rae **released** her **debut** album. It is called *Tug of War*. Popular songs on the album included "Tug of War" and "Bucket."

New Sound

"Call Me Maybe" is known for its catchy dance beat.

Carly Rae gained many fans in Canada as she kept writing music and **performing**. She also began to get new ideas from other bands. She liked music that got people dancing.

So, Carly Rae started to change her music. Her songs began to have a fun pop sound. In 2011, Carly Rae **released** the song "Call Me Maybe" in Canada. It was the first single from her short album *Curiosity*.

Big Break

"Call Me Maybe" gained many fans, including Justin Bieber. He heard the song while visiting Canada. Justin shared it with his fans. By summer 2012, the song was a hit around the world. Millions of people were listening to it online and on the radio.

Carly Rae was excited to work with Justin. She says he helped her become more successful.

17

Internet Sensation

"Call Me Maybe" became more popular because of YouTube and Twitter. Justin Bieber and Selena Gomez told their fans about the song using Twitter.

In February 2012, Justin Bieber, Selena Gomez, Carlos Pena, and others shared a video on YouTube. In it, they pretended to sing "Call Me Maybe." Katy Perry, Cookie Monster, and other stars have made similar videos. YouTube helped Carly Rae's music take off!

Carlos Pena (*left*) is a member of Big Time Rush. Band members Logan Henderson (*second from left*) and Kendall Schmidt (*right*) also appeared in the "Call Me Maybe" YouTube video.

YouTube also helped Justin Bieber become popular. He was discovered after posting videos of himself singing.

Like Carly Rae, Katy Perry is known for her fun dance music.

Crossing Over

In February 2012, Carly Rae had signed a record deal with Justin Bieber and Scooter Braun. She was excited! This helped her music get heard in the United States and around the world.

By June, "Call Me Maybe" was number one on iTunes. And, it spent nine weeks at number one on the Billboard Hot 100.

Fans often ask for Carly Rae's autograph.

Growing Success

In fall 2012, Carly Rae **released** *Kiss*. Fans were excited for this album. It included a **duet** with Justin Bieber called "Beautiful." There was also a song with Owl City called "Good Time."

In summer 2012, Carly Rae performed with Owl City on *Today*.

A Singer's Life

As a singer and songwriter, Carly Rae spends time working on her songs. She writes music and advances her skills. She records songs for her albums at studios.

After her songs come out, Carly Rae works hard to **promote** them. She travels on concert tours and performs live for fans. She poses for pictures with fans and for magazines.

Off the Stage

Carly Rae travels a lot for work. She enjoys seeing famous sites when she visits new cities. In her free time, she plays chess, listens to jazz music, and enjoys cooking. Carly Rae also spends time with family and friends.

Carly Rae likes to help others. She attends events that raise money for causes, such as education.

In summer 2012, Carly Rae attended Arthur Ashe Kids' Day in New York City, New York.

Buzz

In 2013, Carly Rae toured with Justin Bieber. She attended the **Grammy Awards** for the first time. And, she won three **Juno Awards** in Canada.

Carly Rae's fans look forward to what's next for her! Many believe she has a bright **future**.

Carly Rae performed with Australian singer Cody Simpson while on tour in 2013.

Snapshot

★**Name**: Carly Rae Jepsen

★**Birthday**: November 21, 1985

★**Birthplace**: Mission, British Columbia, Canada

★**Appearance**: *Canadian Idol*

★**Albums**: *Tug of War, Curiosity, Kiss*

Important Words

compete to take part in a contest between two or more persons or groups.

debut (DAY-byoo) a first appearance.

duet a song performed by two people.

future (FYOO-chuhr) a time that has not yet occurred.

Grammy Award any of the awards given each year by the National Academy of Recording Arts and Sciences. Grammy Awards honor the year's best accomplishments in music.

guitar (guh-TAHR) a stringed musical instrument played by strumming.

Juno Award any of the awards given each year by the Canadian Academy of Recording Arts and Sciences. Juno Awards honor the year's best accomplishments in music in Canada.

musical a story told with music.

perform to do something in front of an audience.

promote to help something become known.

release to make available to the public.

Web Sites

To learn more about Carly Rae Jepsen, visit ABDO Publishing Company online. Web sites about Carly Rae Jepsen are featured on our Book Links page. These links are routinely monitored and updated to provide the most current information available.

www.abdopublishing.com

Index